CONNECTING RAINBOWS

by

Bob Stanish

illustrated by **Bob Stanish**

Copyright © Good Apple, Inc. 1982

ISBN No. 0-86653-081-9

Printing No. 987

Good Apple, Inc.
Box 299
Carthage, IL 62321-0299

TABLE OF CONTENTS

Table of Contents . . . . ii-iii

Acknowledgements iv

Introduction . . . . v-ix

The Activities

    Future Mirror . . . . 1 - 2

    What's the Most Difficult Thing to Mend? . . . . 3 - 4

    Cooperation Game . . . . 5 - 6

    Wake Up! . . . . 7 - 8

    How Many Different Ways Can You Spell Relief? 9-10

    Quality "Quotes" 11-12

    The Great Improvement Machine 13-14

    Stranded 15-16

    The Good-Feeling Award 17-18

    Star Traits 19-20

    The Sunshine Pop Quiz 21-22

    Improvement Game 23-26

    My Favorite Daydream 27-28

    A Tall Task 29-30

    Time Capsule 31-32

    Survey 33-34

    Inner Warmth 35-36

    Cooperation Squares 37-40

    Flight Patterns 41-42

Some of Your Best Qualities Are 43-44
List Things You'd Feel Like Somersaulting About 45-46
Tangrams 47-48
Time Machine 49-50
List Things That Cause Goose Bumps 51-52
The Green Og 53-54
The Colors of My Rainbow 55-56
The Billboard 57-58
Coauthoring the Story 59-62
Egg-O-Matic 63-64
My Glurp 65-66
List Things That Would Cause Your Knees to Wobble 67-68
My Coat of Arms 69-70
The Misunderstood Monster 71-72
Beat a Bug 73-74
A Three-Person Drawing 75-76
List Things That Are Difficult to Share 77-78
Connecting Rainbows 79-80
The Sunshine Semester Exam 81-82
Bibliography 83-84

ACKNOWLEDGEMENTS

Special thanks to:

Hazel Broughton
Wanda Collins
Pat Connelly
Pat Craig
John Fetter
Pat Hays
Margaret Hokanson
Shirley Hudson
Pam LeMasters
Pat Marinelli
Judy Victor
Theresa Watkin
Vicki White

for their review of the book materials.

A FEW THINGS YOU SHOULD KNOW ABOUT CONNECTING RAINBOWS:

CONNECTING RAINBOWS celebrates living! It's for helping children feel better about themselves, for developing a sensitivity to things, for discovering the worth of cooperations, for learning the value of valuing, and for applying the creative processes more creatively.

WHAT'S THE CONNECTION? "The connection" is that by cultivating FIVE PROCESSES together as a whole a behavioral profile emerges, a profile that can offer GOAL DIRECTION to any classroom teacher for helping students develop more meaning and purpose to their lives.

Look at "The Connection" on page vi. At any given time in your classroom you can easily identify the behavioral concerns of the children you teach. In all probability these concerns are not just manifested in a single category for an individual student. In other words, the concerns are not just a problem with SELF-ESTEEM or lack of VALUES or EMPATHY or COOPERATION or with CREATIVE application. Probably some of the concerns seem to cross process categories. Check this out by thinking of a particular student in your classroom that has caused you concern. Compare the concerns you thought about with the concerns cited in the left-hand column. Chances are three, four, or even five process categories were represented.

Also think of a student you taught whose essence glistened with qualities you admire. Check out these qualities listed under GOALS on "The Connection" page. Again, probably, three or more process categories were represented.

"The Connection" here is rather simple. An interplay of several learning and instructional processes is needed to help students maximize their thinking and feeling potentialities. The most noble truth of all is we can be what we want to be. We were really never meant to be otherwise. Our experiences sometimes hinder this fact. And to a large extent, our experiences determine the kind of person we are. Since learning is an experience, we can learn to be creative, sociable, receptive, responsible and confident. We can also learn to be withdrawn, indifferent, unfeeling, disruptive and dull.

Since experiences affect to a large extent WHO WE ARE and WHAT WE CAN BE, they also can tell us WHAT WE WANT TO BE. By using extending and connecting processes, like the five cited, explanations can be provided for these three extremely important statements.

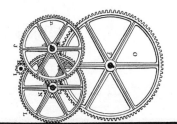

THE CONNECTION

CONCERNS _____ GOALS

UNSURE	**SELF-ESTEEM**	CONFIDENT
CONFUSED	**(PRIDE IN ONESELF)**	PURPOSEFUL
WITHDRAWN		ACTIVE

POSTPONES		DECISIVE
COMPULSIVE	**VALUING**	STEADY
INDIFFERENT	**(CHOOSING, PRIZING, AND ACTING)**	CARING
UNRELIABLE		RESPONSIBLE

CLOSED		OPEN
RESISTENT	**EMPATHY**	RECEPTIVE
UNFEELING	**(SENSITIVITY TO SELF, OTHERS AND EVENTS)**	AWARE

DISRUPTIVE		SUPPORTIVE
NONPARTICIPATING	**COOPERATION**	CONTRIBUTING
ARGUMENTATIVE	**(GETTING ALONG WITH OTHERS; PARTICIPATING)**	SOCIABLE

DULL		IMAGINATIVE
GIVES UP	**THE CREATIVE FACTORS**	CHALLENGES
HESITANT	**(FLUENCY, FLEXIBILITY,**	COURAGEOUS
APATHETIC	**ELABORATION AND ORIGINALITY**	CURIOUS

0 _____ 3 _____ 5 _____ 7 _____ 10

NEGATIVE _____ POSITIVE

HOW TO CONNECT WITH THE ACTIVITIES

It is important that a few general rules be established for **CONNECTING RAINBOWS**. Follow these simple guidelines for making the best use of the activities:

1. ACCEPT! It is important that a climate exists where FEELINGS and THOUGHTS are shared without criticism. Find something of value with written responses and drawings and encourage students WITH PRAISE whenever possible.

2. ASK QUESTIONS to find reasons, to clarify, to generate other alternatives and to stimulate thinking.

3. HAVE FUN with the activities. Don't grade them.

4. SELECT activities that seem to fit a particular reason or situation. TRY FOR THE TEACHABLE MOMENT.

5. YOU PARTICIPATE, TOO! Your participation in the realm of thinking, feeling and doing will be welcomed.

ONE MORE THING ABOUT THE ACTIVITIES

Each STUDENT ACTIVITY PAGE is designed for duplication. Use the activities with the entire class, small groups or individuals. Most of the activities are ideally suited for take-home projects. Encourage students to share their responses with their parents. The processes involved are associated with all aspects of a student's life - especially the home.

A TEACHER DIRECTIONS PAGE accompanies each student activity page. Each teacher directions page has the following sections:

CULTIVATING. . . one or more of the five processes that the activity is promoting.

GETTING STARTED. . . some guidelines for approaching and beginning the activity.

AFTERWARDS. . . ways to broaden the activity concept, follow up on the results and encourage application, if needed.

The teacher suggestions are merely "starters" for you. Your use of them is optional. You are encouraged to expand them, add to them, or revise them in any way. The important thing is the fusion of the processes into daily living for a better life.

MAKING CONNECTIONS WITH THE PROCESSES

Become familiar with these FIVE PROCESSES:

SELF-ESTEEM means . . . . .   feeling proud, having the confidence to get things done, active and purposeful in the pursuit of things.

SELF-ESTEEM is extremely important to the acquisition of knowledge because how well we learn and apply information is directly related to how we feel about ourselves.

VALUING means . . . .   prizing and cherishing those elements in our lives that are special and important. Those elements may include family, friends, and beliefs. In developing new values, the process involves choosing freely, prizing the choice made and acting on it consistently.

VALUING is important to who we are. Values provide the integrity by which we govern our lives. Valuing can cause us to be decisive in our decisions, steady and consistent in our behavior, caring in our attitude and responsible in what we do.

Adapted from **Values and Teaching,** by Louis E. Raths, Merrill Harmin and Sidney B. Simon, Charles E. Merrill Publishing Company, 1966.

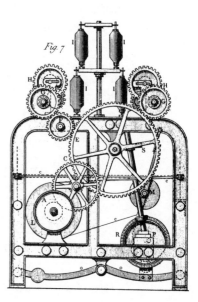

EMPATHY means . . . . . .   tuning into self and others, being sensitive to conditions and events, being open and receptive as opposed to closed and resisting, being able to emotionally feel.

EMPATHY is important to intuiting. It adds to our understanding of events and conditions that affect our lives.

COOPERATION means . . .   developing a working and/or social rapport with others, actively participating, sharing in the process of decision making.

COOPERATION is important because giving and receiving is basic to the welfare of all communities - home, provincial, national or universal.

CREATIVITY means . . . .   improving things. It is the act of generating ideas, refining them and putting them to use-sometimes in varied and unique ways.

CREATIVITY is embodied in four intellectual processes. They are:

FLUENCY. . . . the production of a large number of ideas, products or plans.

FLEXIBILITY. . . . the production of ideas or products that show a variety of possibilities or realms of thought.

ORIGINALITY. . . . the production of ideas that are unique or unusual.

ELABORATION. . . . the production of ideas that display intensive detail or enrichment.

CREATIVITY is important because it is basic human expression.

The four creative factors were identified by E. Paul Torrance in the book, **Guiding Creative Talent**, Prentice-Hall, 1962.

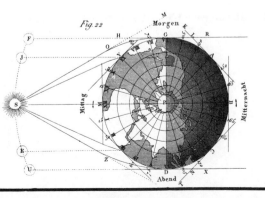

DEDICATION

This book is dedicated to The Velveteen Rabbit and The Little Prince.

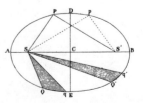

FUTURE MIRROR

CULTIVATING: Self-esteem and Empathy

How we would like others to perceive us is, in a sense, goal setting. Our feelings of self-worth are enhanced when our positive perceptions of self coincide with the perceptions that others have of us.

GETTING STARTED: Encourage students to draw their future portraits from the waist up on the activity sheet. Have them think how they might stylize a shirt, blouse, or coat in a way that might indicate future plans or dreams.

Do not have students sign their names on their individual activity sheets. Upon completion, collect the portraits and place them on a table or tape them to the chalkboard. Place different numbers on each portrait and have each student list on paper the number and the name he thinks the image is.

CAUTION: This activity might identify very graphically those students with poor self-concepts. This, should it occur, will be valuable information to know. Feature some of these students in those activities in this book that focus on "self-esteem through group participation."

AFTERWARDS: Have a general class discussion on the importance of getting to know people. Emphasize that in order to know someone that person must be willing to share of herself or himself. Long or lasting friendships occur this way. Friendship is a commodity that is important to all of us. Friends can help us feel better about ourselves.

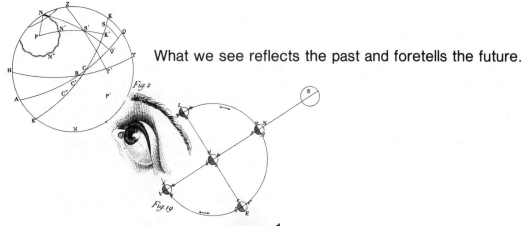

What we see reflects the past and foretells the future.

1

FUTURE MIRROR

Draw yourself in the mirror as you would like others to see you 15 years from now.

WHAT'S THE MOST DIFFICULT THING TO MEND?

CULTIVATING: Valuing and Empathy

Emotional hurt may have a far greater intensity and impact than physical hurt. Learning to deal with it isn't easy, for how we feel about things has a tremendous effect on what we do and how well we do it.

Knowing that others experience emotional problems from time to time is worth knowing for a youngster. While experiencing feelings of this kind, at least there is some understanding that others have gone through it and, usually, the condition is only transitory.

GETTING STARTED: Distribute the activity and allow time for completion.

It is suggested that little information is provided. There may be some students listing physical or object kinds of mending. Just let it be, because the discussion period afterwards should be the real essence of the exercise.

Encourage students to share what the most difficult things to mend would be for them.

AFTERWARDS: Use the opportunity, after the sharing, to get into the concept of emotional hurt. In all probability several students will cite hurts of this type which you could expand on with sensitivity and meaning.

Expand on the notion that in many cases disappointments can become opportunities. Sometimes because of losing we become winners. Look for examples of this in biographies or autobiographies of famous people.

WHAT'S THE MOST DIFFICULT THING TO MEND?

what would it be?

why?

COOPERATION GAME

CULTIVATING: Cooperation and Empathy

Group cooperation can be an expedient way of getting things done.

This exercise will demonstrate dramatically the need for and the use of cooperative teamwork in realizing a group goal. Empathy is involved because a team effort requires a sensitivity to individual team members.

GETTING STARTED: Divide your class into groups of eight to fourteen students. Follow the directions on the activity page and provide time for all groups to complete the exercise.

Note: There may be, from time to time, a group who will require much more time to complete the exercise. If at all possible allow time for a group of this type to complete the task or rearrange the hand entanglement and give them a fresh start.

Observe the groups on the basis of cooperative effort.

AFTERWARDS: Discuss with students the exercise and how the problem caused a cooperative effort by all group members.

Stress the importance of cooperation in group or commitee functions. Make the CONNECTION of this simple exercise to the implementation of any great idea. An idea is only an idea until it is realized. The realization often requires cooperation of others who, to some degree, empathized with the idea or notion.

At times, during the school year when committee or group work becomes stymied by personality or issue conflicts, reintroduce this exercise or verbally recall it as an example of what is required in group cooperation.

COOPERATION GAME

Form a closed circle, shoulder to shoulder of eight to fourteen persons. With arms outstretched toward the center of the circle, everyone takes within his grasp the hand of a different person. A tangle of arms and hands should result which bonds the group together.

Without breaking hand contact, the group should attempt to untangle itself so that a circle results in which hands are held in a normal side-by-side position.

Note: some persons may be facing into the circle, while others are facing out after the untanglement. This is permissible as is verbal communication among group members during the exercise.

WAKE UP!

CULTIVATING: Creativity (originality and elaboration) and Empathy

Finding new uses for things calls for inventiveness. It's a quality that is worth cultivating and one that has carryover to every realm of endeavor.

Finding a new use for something also requires a certain sensitivity to the object or event under investigation. This is, in part, how things are improved - even to the extent of improving self.

GETTING STARTED: This activity is self-explanatory. Encourage students to either describe a solution in writing or to illustrate one. In either case, the solution should be inventive.

AFTERWARDS: Provide time for individual explanations as to the solutions to the problem.

Complete the exercise in an upbeat fashion by asking students to list things not worth getting out of bed for.

Make CONNECTIONS with student drawings or descriptions to the concept of cause and effect. Make further CONNECTIONS with scientific discovery, with economic changes, with world hunger or with almost everything. In other words, paraphrasing what Newton said, "for every action there's a reaction" CONNECTS to human experiences on all realms.

Greet the morning sun each and every day.

WAKE UP!

Devise a way to get up in the a.m. without an alarm clock or wake-up call.

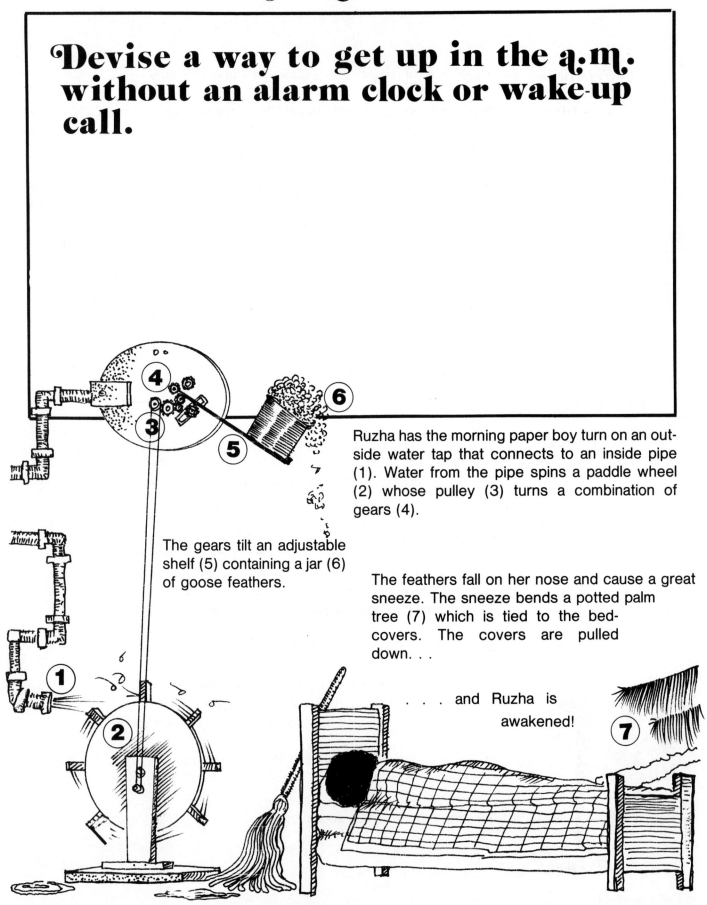

Ruzha has the morning paper boy turn on an outside water tap that connects to an inside pipe (1). Water from the pipe spins a paddle wheel (2) whose pulley (3) turns a combination of gears (4).

The gears tilt an adjustable shelf (5) containing a jar (6) of goose feathers.

The feathers fall on her nose and cause a great sneeze. The sneeze bends a potted palm tree (7) which is tied to the bed-covers. The covers are pulled down. . .

. . . and Ruzha is awakened!

CULTIVATING: Creativity (originality and elaboration) and Empathy

Finding new uses for things calls for inventiveness. It's a quality that is worth cultivating and one that has carryover to every realm of endeavor.

Finding a new use for something also requires a certain sensitivity to the object or event under investigation. This is, in part, how things are improved - even to the extent of improving self.

GETTING STARTED: This activity is self-explanatory. Encourage students to either describe a solution in writing or to illustrate one. In either case, the solution should be inventive.

AFTERWARDS: Provide time for individual explanations as to the solutions to the problem.

Complete the exercise in an upbeat fashion by asking students to list things not worth getting out of bed for.

Make CONNECTIONS with student drawings or descriptions to the concept of cause and effect. Make further CONNECTIONS with scientific discovery, with economic changes, with world hunger or with almost everything. In other words, paraphrasing what Newton said, "for every action there's a reaction" CONNECTS to human experiences on all realms.

Greet the morning sun each and every day.

WAKE UP!

Devise a way to get up in the a.m. without an alarm clock or wake-up call.

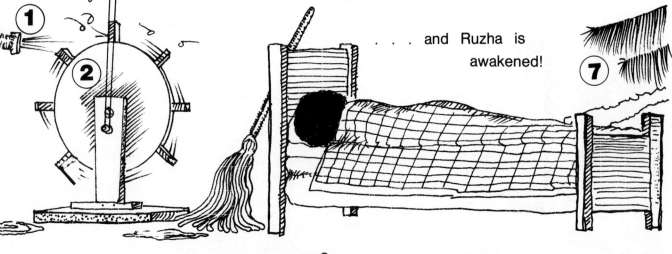

Ruzha has the morning paper boy turn on an outside water tap that connects to an inside pipe (1). Water from the pipe spins a paddle wheel (2) whose pulley (3) turns a combination of gears (4).

The gears tilt an adjustable shelf (5) containing a jar (6) of goose feathers.

The feathers fall on her nose and cause a great sneeze. The sneeze bends a potted palm tree (7) which is tied to the bedcovers. The covers are pulled down. . .

. . . and Ruzha is awakened!

HOW MANY DIFFERENT WAYS CAN YOU SPELL RELIEF?

CULTIVATING:

Creativity (fluency and flexibility) and Valuing

It is important to develop verbal fluency. Idea quantity is a necessary process before qualitative ideas emerge.

GETTING STARTED:

Use this fun-approach activity as a means of helping students generate ideas.

Provide about ten minutes of writing time and if more space is needed, encourage students to use the backsides of their activity sheets.

Have students think about the many aspects of their lives (flexibility) in responding to the question.

AFTERWARDS:

Ask for students to volunteer some of their responses.

Have students cite their greatest relief as asked for on the activity page.

Develop empathy with other occupations by asking questions like:

"How might a farmer spell relief?"
"How might a disc jockey spell relief?"
"How might a dentist spell relief?"

Make other CONNECTIONS like:

"How might a hungry person spell relief?"
"How might a lonely person spell relief?"
"How might an endangered species spell relief?"

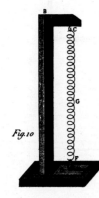

With the above, encourage as many different spellings as possible. In what ways might some of the spellings be solutions?

How many different ways can you spell RELIEF?

recess

The greatest relief is _____

because _____

_____

_____ .

QUALITY "QUOTES"

CULTIVATING: Self-esteem and Valuing

To a great extent what we're told we are, we become. This notion carries a number of limitations if what we're told is continuously negative. The real truth of the matter is that we can become what we want to become. The beginning point is to determine what we want.

GETTING STARTED: Encourage students to visualize both faces and names of people they admire. Afterwards, have them focus on specific qualities these people have, qualities they admire.

Tell students that after they complete the activity you would like to see their responses. Don't share the results with the class.

AFTERWARDS: As a class determine what the most important human traits are.

Encourage students to compare the quotes they cited with the class listing.

When you have the activity responses in hand, look for clues by which you can help students become what they want to become. This information will be invaluable in those moments when a compliment by you will not only carry the impact of the situation but a more significant meaning as well.

Legacies are begun with words.

11

QUALITY "QUOTES"

Think of people you admire.
Think of their qualities which earned your respect.

You probably have many of the same qualities, perhaps all of them.

The people below are talking about you!

What would you like them to say?

THE GREAT IMPROVEMENT MACHINE

CULTIVATING: Valuing

Self-improvement focuses on the things we consider important, the things we value and the intensity of personal commitment.

Establishing personal goals is the most important element to personal growth.

GETTING STARTED: Encourage students to think about things they have improved on over the past few years. Also encourage them to think about the things they consider important and not necessarily what others consider important. In other words personal expectations and personal achievements are the things to consider. These thoughts should be listed in the section "Stuff I've had in" on the activity sheet.

Tell students to take several minutes and just think about areas in their lives that could use improvement - things they consider to be important. These thoughts should be listed in the "Stuff to put in" section of the activity sheet.

AFTERWARDS: Share the improvements and the things to be improved.

Have students examine the illustration and respond to how the drawing illustrates the act of improvement. Improvement generally goes through a lot of channels and sometimes it gets murky. Improvement is not a simple process. It takes time, commitment and work. Ask, "Why is it important to always think about the stuff to put in?"

For additional follow-up, try some of these open-ended statements:

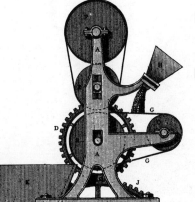

I used to be _____, but now I'm
_____.

Now I'm _____, but I'd like to be
_____.

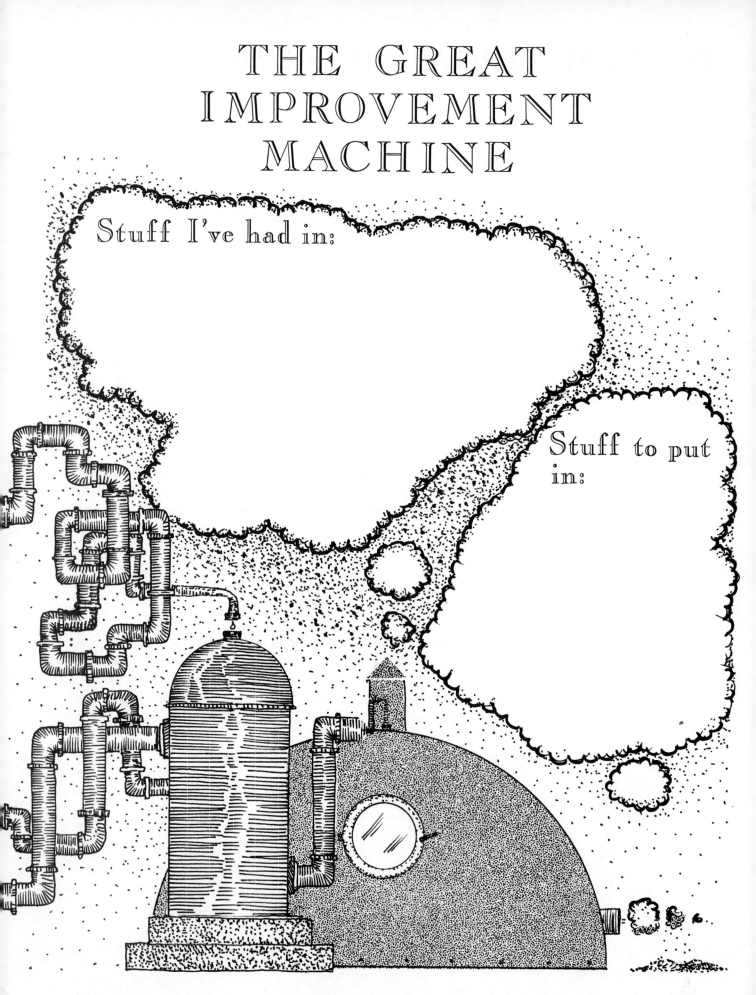

THE GREAT IMPROVEMENT MACHINE

Stuff I've had in:

Stuff to put in:

STRANDED

CULTIVATING: Cooperation and Creativity (flexibility)

Arriving at consensus through compromise is a basic exercise in democracy.

Creative approaches to problems can facilitate cooperation and compromise.

GETTING STARTED: Form groups of four to five students for this exercise.

The flexibility in this activity is in the creative approach to selecting the discarded items. Don't announce this. Just allow the groups to discover this on their own.

AFTERWARDS: Allow a spokesman from each group to explain how they approached the problem and how they arrived at their choices.

Make CONNECTIONS with the exercise and group decision making on:

. . . family budget making,

. . . governmental decision making,

. . . and any organization that has to deal with limited funds, available time, and varying opinions and attitudes within.

There are moments in our lives when we all feel **STRANDED.** What is needed, in all cases, is creative resourcefulness.

STRANDED

Your group will be stranded on an island in the Pacific Ocean. The island is uninhabited by people but has adequate plant and animal life. You have only $275.00 with which to buy some of the supplies listed below. Decide as a group what to buy!

item:	amount:
	$
	$
	$
	$
	$
	$
	$

total: $

Behind the tent and yours for the asking:

8 empty oil drums (50 gal. size)
60 ft. of old heavy-duty rope
a broken anchor
an oil drum of rusty nails

Inside the tent:

6-volt battery lantern $25.00
8 sleeping bags at $45.00 each
2 hardwood oars: $25.00
fishing pole and fully-equipped tackle
    box: $50.00
hunting bow and arrows: $175.00
hunting knife: $25.00

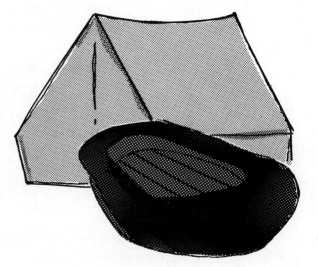

And   one 6-person nylon wall tent: $125.00
       one 3-person vinyl boat: $250.00

THE GOOD-FEELING AWARD

CULTIVATING: Valuing and Self-esteem

Acclaiming what we prize and cherish may be the beginning of or a value system itself. Having values enables us to be more self-reliant and purposeful in our daily lives.

GETTING STARTED: Set aside a few minutes every few weeks for this activity. The concept of the activity is to encourage student pride concerning those things or events that have had a positive effect on their daily lives. "The Good-Feeling Award" might go to a parent, a sister or brother, a friend, a newsworthy event or whatever. The important thing is to publically acclaim in a classroom some meaningful event in our lives.

When introducing this activity for the first time, provide plenty of help. Discuss with students what kinds of things cause good feelings. Accept the material gift sort of thing but extend the concept to include the meaning of friendship, words of thoughtfulness and support, cooperating and acts of kindness.

The second time the activity is completed will produce a more meaningful response. Give students a week's notice before you do the activity so that adequate time is available for thinking and planning. Also provide the option of passing. Sometimes a whole week can go bad!

AFTERWARDS: Try to establish a committee of students to determine how the award might be presented to another class or to another student in a different class or to school personnel for something they did that benefited others in the school.

Encourage the principal to use "The Good-Feeling Award" for things he or she would like to commend in the school.

THE GOOD-FEELING AWARD

To: ....

For: ....

....

....

....

This is a Good-feeling Award. Think of people or events you could give it to.

STAR TRAITS

CULTIVATING: Valuing

Identifying what we admire in others can be goals for our own self-improvement.

GETTING STARTED: Inform students that they should take their time in listing the five people they admire. They can consider fictional characters from books, historical figures from the past or present or people they know.

The personality traits they associate with the five people are to be listed, then ranked according to importance. Let each student determine what traits are the most important or the least important.

AFTERWARDS: After sharing their lists, encourage students to make CONNECTIONS with the listed traits and the traits they would consider most important for a politician to have, a banker to have, a teacher to have, a physician to have, and an attorney to have. Do this by saying: "On your list of traits which trait would be most important for a politician to have? A banker to have?" etc.

All life forms have traits to be admired.
It's just a matter of finding the right traits.

STAR TRAITS

1 _____
2 _____
3 _____
4 _____
5 _____

Which five people, past or present, real or fiction, do you admire the MOST?

Suppose you could mold their qualities together to form a very SPECIAL PERSON!

DO IT BY LISTING THEIR SPECIAL TRAITS HERE:

RANK

1 _____ ➡ ☐
2 _____ ➡ ☐
3 _____ ➡ ☐
4 _____ ➡ ☐
5 _____ ➡ ☐
6 _____ ➡ ☐
7 _____ ➡ ☐
8 _____ ➡ ☐
9 _____ ➡ ☐
10 _____ ➡ ☐

Now rank the traits by their importance, 1 (highest) thru 10 (lowest).

My best trait is _____.

Something else about me is _____
_____
_____
_____.

THE SUNSHINE POP QUIZ

CULTIVATING: Valuing

Life can be a learning experience in whatever we do. Knowing what we prize and cherish can be an important aid in the processing of new information.

GETTING STARTED: Use this activity at the end of a school day throughout the school year.

Allow time for completion, but warn students you will ask them to read their statements. Indicate that not all learning occurs in the classroom and that their statements may reflect on events outside the classroom.

AFTERWARDS: Before the statements are read indicate that no reaction from others should occur. The statements should be read without comment.

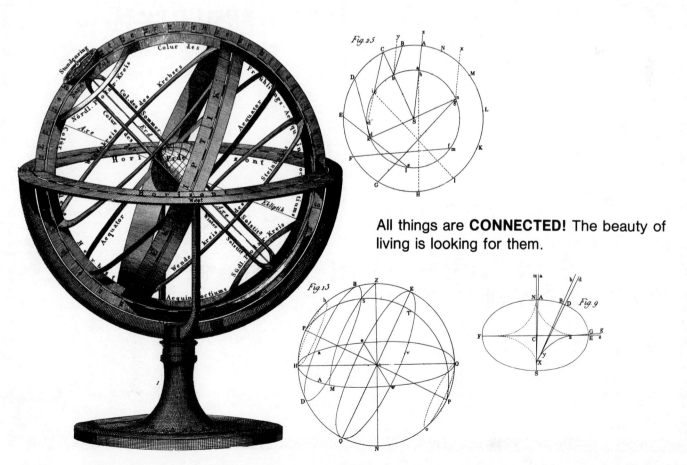

All things are **CONNECTED!** The beauty of living is looking for them.

THE SUNSHINE POP QUIZ

name: date:

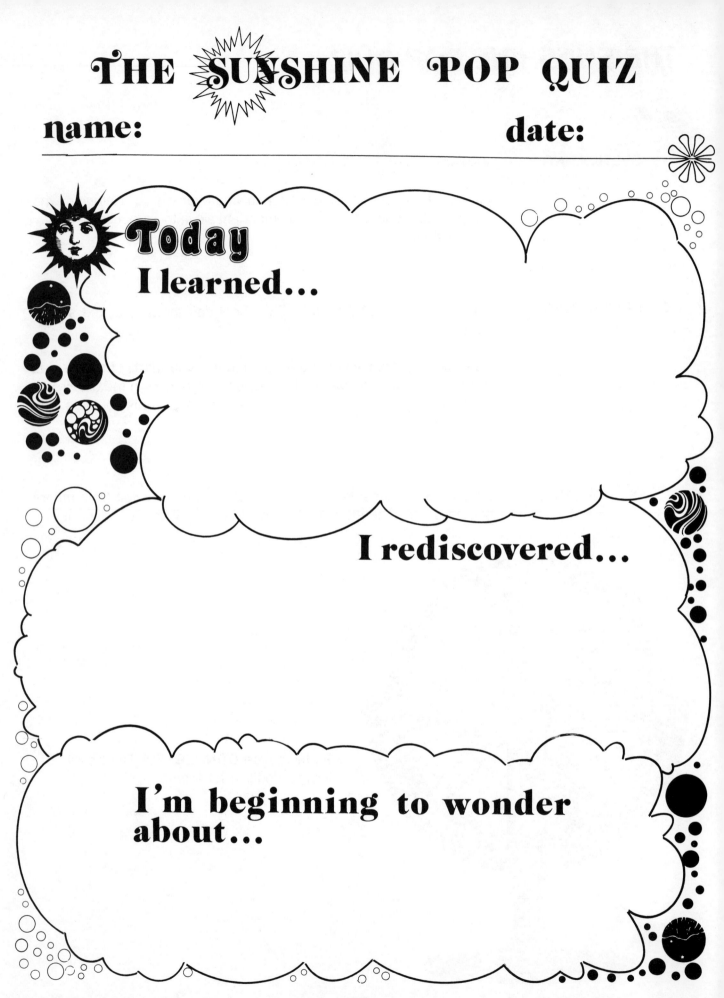

Today
I learned...

I rediscovered...

I'm beginning to wonder
about...

IMPROVEMENT GAME

CULTIVATING:　　　Cooperation and Creativity (originality and elaboration)

There is a CONNECTION bond between almost all things, maybe even all things. Sometimes we might have to force a fit (connection), but it's there.

The creative process itself involves different arrangements of the ordinary for fresh insights and new CONNECTIONS for improving things.

GETTING STARTED:　　This activity will generate discovery and excitement and a glimpse into the inventive processes.

Read the directions for the "Improvement Game" and have ready the various materials called for in the activity.

Although you could go either way on this activity, try giving the item to be improved last.

AFTERWARDS:　　　Provide plenty of time for the sharing of the improved product along with the commercial statements.

TRY: . 　.　 .　 . 　. 　doing this concept with new content words at the beginning of a unit. In other words force-fit the function of terms like New Deal, square root, adjective or anything on to the product to be improved.

. 　.　 .　 . 　. 　doing this as a means of teaching word comprehension.

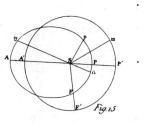

. 　.　 .　 . 　. 　doing this as a means of improving things such as a faculty meeting, a playground, a resource room or whatever.

23

IMPROVEMENT GAME

DIRECTIONS:

1   Duplicate two copies of page 25 and as many copies as you will have groups of four to five students of page 26. Cut along the dotted lines on page 25 so that card-sized pieces of paper will result.

2   Distribute to each group three pieces of paper from page 25. Each piece of paper given to each group should have a different word. Different groups may have the same word. Also distribute to each group one copy of page 26.

TELL STUDENTS:

3   Most words have multiple meanings. In small groups decide what particular meaning they would like for each of their words. Write this meaning on the appropriate piece of paper. Using the dictionary is permissible.

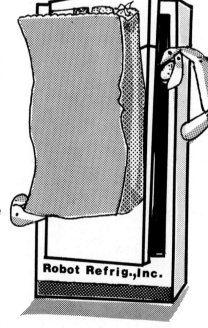

4   To decide on what it is that's going to be improved. It is suggested that you begin with a refrigerator, a grocery shopping cart, or a mailbox. At a later time try almost any object. Anything with a function will work. Also try different words.

5   To force-fit the function of the word meaning on to the item to be improved.

6   To share findings by writing a commercial for the improved item.

X RAY

word meaning:

ABSORB

word meaning:

CONVEYER

word meaning:

INDEX

word meaning:

INTAKE

word meaning:

TRUMPET

word meaning:

ZIP CODE

word meaning:

ARM

word meaning:

INFLATE

word meaning:

SIGNAL

word meaning:

25

IMPROVEMENT GAME

Write each word in one of these   On the lines provided, describe
how the word's meaning would function to improve the item.

Write a commercial for the improved item.

MY FAVORITE DAYDREAM

CULTIVATING: Valuing

Daydreams and fantasies can be goal-setting devices. They generally consist of the things we would like to see happen.

GETTING STARTED: Ask students to think about some of their daydreams. Have them think about the ones that seem to occur again and again.

Distribute the activity sheets and provide time for completion. Indicate to students that time will be allowed for everyone to share a daydream description with the entire class.

AFTERWARDS: Provide time for the sharing of the daydreams. Look for descriptions that deal with future aspirations. You might make a few clarifying statements during the readings like:

"Is this something you'd really like to see happen? In what ways would the reality of this dream be important to you?"

"In making this daydream a reality, what kinds of things would you need to do?"

"In what ways would this daydream be of value to you if it became true?"

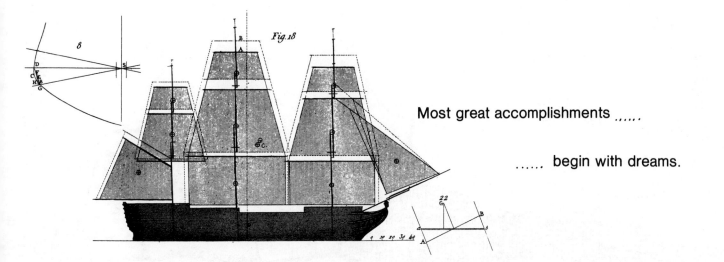

Most great accomplishments ......

...... begin with dreams.

MY FAVORITE DAYDREAM

IS--

A TALL TASK

CULTIVATING: Cooperation and Creativity (fluency, flexibility and originality)

Exercising creative thinking in group or committee work is a common function in many businesses and industries. Ideas cause other ideas to occur. Cooperative creating is a way many innovations begin.

GETTING STARTED: Divide your class into groups of four or five students. Provide a copy of the student activity sheet to each group.

Explain to students that good ideas are usually the result of many ideas. Encourage each group to generate as many ideas as possible, using as much paper as necessary.

Also indicate to students that once the ideas have been generated, there will be a need to determine how the three best ideas should be chosen. Encourage students to think of ways they can evaluate the ideas. Suggest that cost factors, practicality, multi-purposes or functions of the gadgets, etc., are things they might consider using to determine the three best ideas. There are many other ways (criteria) in addition to those, but the important thing is to use some standard for determining a selection.

Provide twenty minutes for activity completion.

AFTERWARDS: Ask a representative from each group to present their findings and their name for the product. Also ask for the criteria or standards by which they rated their ideas.

Do mock television commercials on the improved product; then discuss the impact of the media on commercial products. In what ways might consumers assess the value of products prior to purchase?

If Thomas Edison was alive, what kinds of inventions might he be working on today? In what ways is it important for all of us to be adaptable and flexible in our own lives?

A TALL TASK

You and your group are employed in the Research and Development Section of Sports International, Inc. One product the company manufactured was the EASY KNEE-SAVER for tall basketball players. The product was to save on the off-the-court wear and tear of the knees of these athletes by picking up things they drop, tying shoe-strings, etc. The product has sold poorly, so the company has added two additional plugs for two additional gadgets.

Management now feels the product may have a brighter future in other markets than sports.

As members of the Research and Development Section, think of what other gadgets the product might accommodate and what uses they could perform. Select the three best ideas and rename the product.

30

TIME CAPSULE

CULTIVATING: Valuing

To affirm something consistently and to act accordingly is a value. It's as simple as that! Not having values is to live life postponing things, being compulsive rather than consistent, being indifferent rather than caring and unreliable rather than responsible. It is not a teacher's role to teach values. It is a teacher's role to help students in becoming more decisive, more consistent, more caring, and more responsible. By doing this students become more value-oriented in developing their own values.

GETTING STARTED: Distribute the activity sheet or make an overhead projector transparency of the activity for group viewing.

Caution students to spend several minutes in analyzing the things they have that they consider important - things that would describe who they are, things that would describe what they care about and things that are of value to them on this day in this year.

AFTERWARDS: Encourage students to share their time capsule items.

Ask students what suggestions they have for placing five items in a time capsule that would represent their class.

How about their community?

How about their nation?

We always time-capsule something of ourselves - for better or worse.

31

TIME CAPSULE

Items: _____ ◈

_____ ◈

_____ ◈

_____ ◈

_____ ◈

There's a crowd gathering to see what you'll place in a time capsule for the year 3000.

CULTIVATING: Valuing

Effective values are timeless. They are the foundation on which life decisions are made, purposeful behavior is directed, and autonomy maintained.

This activity looks for potential value indicators in a broad spectrum of areas. Look for CONNECTIONS on strong beliefs and aspirations which students consider important.

GETTING STARTED: Encourage students to project themselves to the year 2006. Have them consider how old they would be, then quietly reflect on what they might have accomplished from now to that point in future time.

After the reflection period, have students complete the Survey.

AFTERWARDS: Have students share their survey responses. This should create interesting listening and an indication of future aspirations.

Fig. 2

Aspiration is one of the fundamental conditions for growing.

SURVEY

After the year 2000, my greatest accomplishment was

_____

_____

_____

_____.

Other achievements:

_____

_____

_____

_____

_____

_____

_____

_____

_____

_____

September 20, 2006

Name _____ **Age** _____

Address _____

Marital status _____ **Number of children** _____

Type of employment _____

Hobbies & Interests _____

_____

_____

_____

_____

_____

INNER WARMTH

CULTIVATING: Self-esteem, Valuing, Empathy and Creativity (fluency and flexibility)

Knowing and keeping in touch with the things we like is significant. Often, when things are not going well, we can lose sight of the truly important things.

GETTING STARTED: Encourage students to write as many things as they possibly can. Have them fill up the page any way they choose.

AFTERWARDS: Have students do the following:

. . .   Draw a circle around every item that would only require the sense of hearing in order to experience it.

. . .   Draw a rectangle around every item that would require money in order to experience it.

. . .   Draw a triangle around every item that required some effort on an individual's part in order to experience it.

Some items might require a triangle in a rectangle or a triangle in a circle or a circle in a rectangle.

Now ask:

"What shape did you most often use?"

"Think about it for a few minutes and then write an 'I learned . . . ' statement."

Ask students to refer back to their pages and count the items that did not require a shape such as a circle, rectangle, triangle or a combination of two shapes.

Ask for explanations as to why those statements didn't fit a circle, a rectangle, or a triangle? Note: You might receive some highly sensitive visual experiences here, for example, the face of a relative or friend, etc. Should it occur, please allow these kinds of reactions to flow.

INNER WARMTH

THINGS THAT CAN CAUSE ME TO WARM UP ON THE INSIDE:

a compliment

chile

a good grade

COOPERATION SQUARES

CULTIVATING: Cooperation and Empathy

Cooperation can result from competition.

Opportunities will occur in this exercise to directly look at those factors that hinder or assist cooperative effort.

GETTING STARTED: Reproduce the COOPERATION SQUARES on pieces of construction paper or cardboard. There should be enough squares to accommodate each student playing the game. For each team, place assorted pieces of the four squares into four envelopes.

Form the teams of four students. Should there be additional students not included, have them act as observers and recall their observations when the game is completed.

Begin the activity by reading the overview and rules of the game to your students. Tell students that the first team to finish should quietly observe the other teams. Indicate that the rule of no talking would still be in effect. Follow the same procedures with the second team to finish, the third team, etc.

AFTERWARDS: Share your observations of the activity and encourage the observers and others to do so as well. Discuss as a class those factors that hinder or help cooperative effort.

Cooperation is both a thinking and feeling thing.

COOPERATION SQUARES

OVERVIEW

The class is divided into teams of four students. Each team member receives an envelope with some pieces of the puzzle. These pieces must be shared among each team of four so that four completed squares result. All four squares must be the same size.

RULES:

1. The task of each team member is to complete a square directly in front of him or her.

2. Each team member is to work only on his or her square, not on the square of another person.

3. A team member can give pieces to another team member. A team member cannot gesture for pieces unless they are offered.

4. No talking or gesturing is allowed.

5. The first team with all four squares completed is the winner!

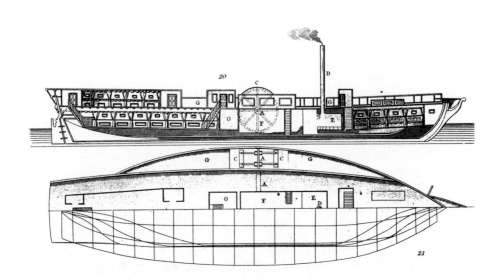

COOPERATION
SQUARES

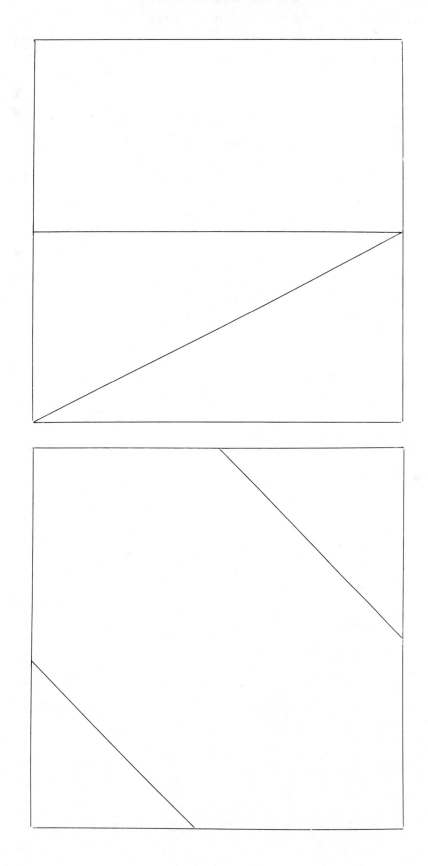

COOPERATION
SQUARES

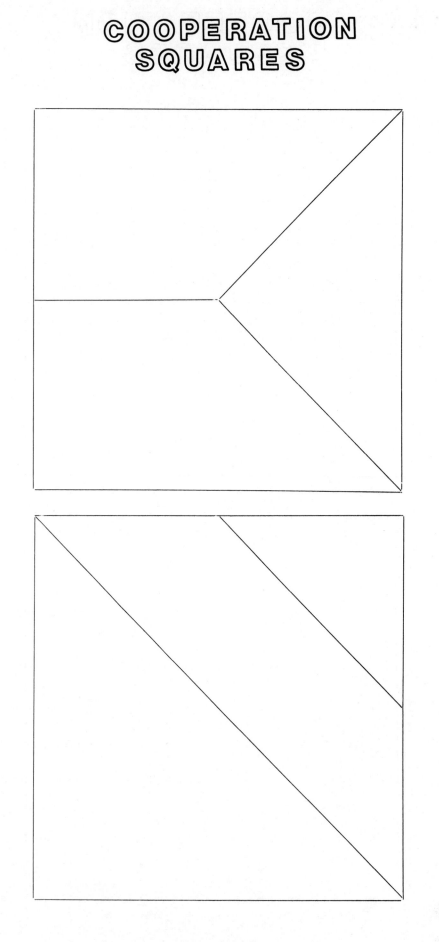

FLIGHT PATTERNS

CULTIVATING: Self-esteem and Empathy

How we perceive ourselves is reflected in what we think, feel and do.

GETTING STARTED: Discuss with your students the various flight patterns on this activity page. One balloon, in the lower right, is going the opposite way-against the wind. One balloon is flying higher, one is leading, and one is following the leader.

Ask your students to identify themselves with one of the balloons in the illustration. "How is that particular balloon most like you?"

AFTERWARDS: Encourage students to share their results with another student. Provide time for each team of two to respond to each other's flight pattern.

Ask some metaphorical questions like:

"How is a hot air balloon like a dictionary?"

Although there are many answers to questions like the above, accept them all. Expect responses like a hot air balloon is like a dictionary because both deal with expansion - expansion of air and expansion of knowledge.

Try other questions like:

"How is a hot air balloon like a hamburger?"

"How is a hot air balloon like a rainbow?"

"How is a hot air balloon like mathematics?"

The greatest value in arriving anywhere
is to appreciate where you've been.

FLIGHT PATTERNS

Which hot air balloon is most like you? ___
Why?

Are you satisfied with your flight pattern?
Explain!

SOME OF YOUR BEST QUALITIES ARE . . .

CULTIVATING: Self-esteem and Empathy

How we think others feel about us is extremely important. Our self-esteem and confidence is strengthened when we feel support and appreciation from others.

GETTING STARTED: Discuss in very general terms what might be described as desirable human qualities or traits. Discussion might encompass such factors as concern or sensitivity to the feelings of others, humor, a special gift or talent, honesty, courage, leadership, causing others to feel better about themselves, etc.

Tell students that today's activity calls for helping others feel better about themselves. Generally, when we feel good about ourselves we do things a little better.

Try with your class one of these two options:

OPTION ONE: Place an activity sheet on the bulletin board with a student's name on it. Leave the activity sheet intact for several days and encourage other students to write positive statements about the student featured. After a few days take down the activity sheet and give it to the student. Repeat the procedure until all students have had an opportunity to be featured.

OPTION TWO: Divide your class into groups of five or six students. Have each student pin an activity sheet to his/her blouse or shirt. On small pieces of paper, have students write a positive statement about each group member. Statements are to be taped to each activity sheet. Activity sheets are then unpinned and read silently.

AFTERWARDS: As a class, determine what the best qualities of friendship are? Try it with leadership or team play or inventiveness or CONNECT it with some other human trait.

Some of your best qualities are...

LIST THINGS
YOU'D FEEL LIKE SOMERSAULTING ABOUT

CULTIVATING: Valuing and Cooperation

An overt demonstration of joy is an infectious thing. It can be contagious both to observers and those involved. Usually the things we really enjoy are embodied with values or value indicators.

GETTING STARTED: Encourage students to list all of the things they can think of that would normally make them happy. Should more space be needed, have them use the backsides of their activity pages. Provide about ten minutes or so for completion.

AFTERWARDS: Ask students to check the items on their lists that would normally require another individual or friends to do. In other words, the items requiring some degree of cooperation from someone else or others should be checked.

Ask students to count the checked responses for cooperative effort and the ones unchecked.

Ask if the comparison between the counts of the unchecked and their checked responses would tell them anything about themselves?

Encourage students to share the things they'd feel like somersaulting about with the entire class.

It takes a little cooperation to arrive at any destination.

LIST THINGS YOU'D FEEL LIKE SOMERSAULTING ABOUT

1
2
3
4
5
6
7

Underline the happiest somersault!

TANGRAMS

CULTIVATING: Creativity (originality, flexibility and elaboration) and Cooperation

Creativity can easily flow through structure, even highly-structured ones.

Cooperation deals, in part, with anticipating the needs of others.

GETTING STARTED: AS AN INDIVIDUAL EXERCISE in creativity (originality), distribute a complete tangram set to each student. A complete set would consist of seven numbered polygons (see next page). Ask students to create a picture of something creative and original. Also indicate that, hopefully, their picture would be something no one else would think of, but that others would recognize. All seven pieces must be used. Tangrams can be arranged to represent ideas, animals, objects or a person.

AS A GROUP EXERCISE IN COOPERATIVE EFFORT, provide a tangram set to teams of two students. Individual teams must take turns in assembling the idea, animal, object or person being represented. NO COMMUNICATION is permitted during the exercise, and after each assembled picture, a rough sketch of the picture is drawn by a team member. The tangram pieces are then rearranged to form a different picture. Provide a fifteen minute time limit and encourage teams to construct as many concepts as possible.

AFTERWARDS: When the INDIVIDUAL EXERCISE is used, check for one-of-a-kind pictures for originality.

 When the GROUP EXERCISE is used, check for flexibility of thinking by counting the different categories of thought displayed, check for originality by identifying the "one-of-a-kind" responses and check for fluency by counting the quantity of pictures created per team.

TANGRAMS

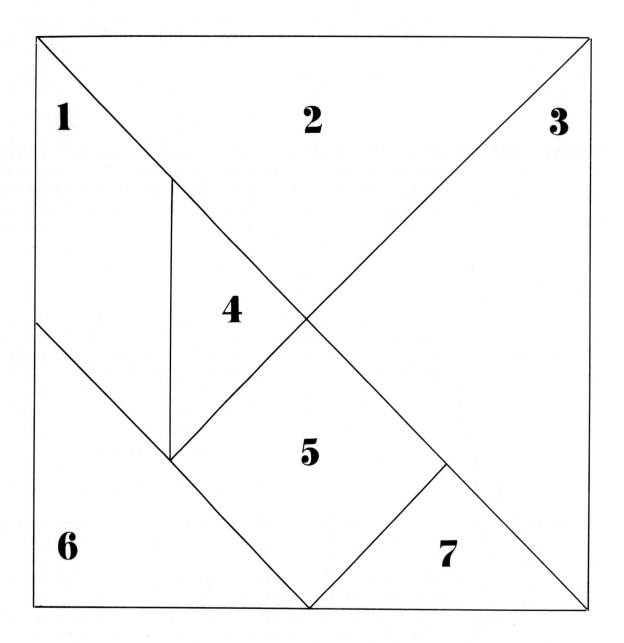

TIME MACHINE

CULTIVATING: Valuing and Empathy

Although we can never reconstruct hindsight for another try, it is of value to reexamine situations that gave us a "fork in the road" choice, for no other reason but for the simple rediscovery that there are alternatives to most situations that require decision making.

GETTING STARTED: Begin this activity by focusing attention on the thought that humans are human - that we are not machines and that all of us make mistakes. We shouldn't spend a lifetime examining our mistakes. But it is of importance to go back in time and recall situations for the purpose of examining the process we used in making a decision. Knowing how to evaluate choices is a skill that can be cultivated.

Distribute the activity sheets and allow students time for completion.

AFTERWARDS: During the sharing period direct your questioning in a mode of clarification:

"Did you have other choices? What were they?"

"What might have been the result of these choices?"

"Might you have more choices now than when the problem presented itself? In what ways?"

"In what ways might you evaluate choices?"

It's the time you spend on things that matters,
not the time it takes.

49

 IME MACHINE

Time-machine yourself back in time and do something differently for some better results!

What would it be?

How?

LIST THINGS THAT CAUSE GOOSE BUMPS

CULTIVATING: Empathy

Excitement is one of the joys of living. All of us, from time to time, internalize the beauty of a certain view, a certain sound or a certain understanding of meaning. Those moments linger in our memories. To have few of these experiences is a tragedy. To touch base with what we had is to expand the senses for more to come.

GETTING STARTED: Recall from your own experiences those . . .

visual images that have lingered in your memory;

sounds of life or of music;

ideas that have lingered, be it forms of action you've taken or dreams that have remained.

Share these experiences of yours with your students.

Allow plenty of time for completion of the activity page. Due to the reflective substance of the material, you might consider having your students take the page home for additional work time.

It is recommended that you tell students that before they write anything to . . .

let their minds wander on sights, sounds, and thoughts of this year and the years preceding;

find a comfortable place away from distractions for the wanderings of their minds;

take one concept at a time. In other words, allow the concept of sight to enter your consciousness first, then sound, and finally thoughts.

AFTERWARDS: Share, share, share . . .! There will be some interesting CONNECTIONS made on the process of sharing.

LIST THINGS
THAT CAUSE GOOSE BUMPS

SIGHTS: _____
_____
_____
_____
_____
_____
_____

SOUNDS: _____
_____
_____
_____
_____

THOUGHTS: _____
_____
_____
_____
_____
_____
_____
_____
_____
_____
_____

THE GREEN OG

CULTIVATING: Empathy and Valuing

External judgment is the most accessible and the easiest method for determining what we like and dislike. But, if given the time and the inclination, an internal view is always far more significant. To discover the value of anything is an empathetic exercise in caring.

;ETTING STARTED: Before students begin to write have them share their initial reactions to the green og.

AFTERWARDS: Encourage students to share what they did with the green og and why?

What if they were the last remaining green og? Would they be satisfied with the solution they gave?

Encourage students to make CONNECTIONS with the green og and . . .

    . . .   persons who are outwardly different from themselves.

    . . .   moments in their own lives when they felt like a green og.

    . . .   cultures and species who are no longer.

    . . .   species that are endangered.

Vision requires more than just seeing.

This is a green og. It's half human and half animal.

The green og is the last of its kind. Some want to destroy it because of its ugliness. Some would buy tickets to see it. Some zoos would love to exhibit it. Some would feature it in horror films, while others want it for medical research.

The green og is given to you!

What will you do with it?

Why?

THE COLORS OF MY RAINBOW

CULTIVATING: Empathy and Valuing

Living causes encounters with feelings. Some feelings we enjoy, but others may cause concern. To accept self and to accept others is to accept a wide spectrum of emotional feelings as a very basic human condition.

GETTING STARTED: Prior to activity work, discuss with students what is expected. This might be best done by offering some examples from your own life similar to the following:

Color me burnt orange when I get into trouble for something someone else did.

Color me gracious green when I loan my record albums to friends.

Color me mellow yellow after a Thanksgiving dinner.

Color me moody blue when a friend is angry with me.

Color me bright red when I forget to bring my gym shoes to P.E. class.

and . . .

another color I am is ***bright yellow** when I receive a compliment from a respected friend.

*Note: Encourage students to think of various tones or color variations on the color they have to come up with.

Encourage students to work independently. Indicate that the sharing of responses afterwards will be voluntary.

One of the values inherent in this activity is that students will realize that events and feelings that may appear only unique to them are rather universal.

AFTERWARDS: Implement the rule of passing. In other words, don't force a student to share a response if he doesn't want to.

Through discussion indicate that all of us experience a variety of emotions. How we handle our emotions is very basic in our relationships with others and to ourselves.

THE COLORS
of my
RAINBOW

Color me ...

burnt orange when I . . .

gracious green when I . . .

mellow yellow when I . . .

moody blue when I . . .

bright red when I . . .

Another color I am is _____ when I . . .

THE BILLBOARD

CULTIVATING: Self-esteem and Creativity (originality)

Learning to share what talents we have is important. Talents are not just competencies. Talents represent modes of learning and ways of looking at things. Knowing our own resources and the resources of others can be the basis for establishing friendships, generating alternative solutions to difficult problems, and finding more effective ways of enjoying life.

GETTING STARTED: Do this as an individual student activity. Encourage students to think of two or three things about themselves that they could advertise. Have students think of jingles, catchy phrases and commercial ads for their billboards. Also, encourage the use of illustrations or cutouts from magazines.

AFTERWARDS: Display student billboards and have students discuss their personal advertisements.

On a large sheet of butcher or wrapping paper, encourage your students to create a "class" billboard using class events and achievements as a starting point.

A caterpillar can look forward to change.
And so can we.
We can be whatever we want to be.

THE BILLBOARD

Create an ad about **YOU!**

COAUTHORING THE STORY

CULTIVATING: Creativity (originality), Empathy, and Cooperation

Being able to identify with situations and individuals outside of our normal realm of experiences is, in a sense, looking at things from different frames of references. More knowledge is gained when we expand our consciousnesses in imaginative ways and in CONNECTING kinds of ways. Therefore, the paradoxes and problems we encounter daily become a little more solvable.

GETTING STARTED: Provide the directions on page 60 of COAUTHORING to your students.

This activity will generate interest. So, don't blow the whistle too soon! You might consider waiting a day before stories are read and shared in class.

AFTERWARDS: Check for originality by noting the use of surprising plots, the use of unusual or unconventional events, unique endings and the use of paradoxes to explain a happening.

Check for empathy by noting the identification of students with the story.

Check for cooperation by noting the ability of your students to work with each other.

Do a follow-up in a week or so by having your students quietly imagine themselves holding on to a giant balloon. Encourage them to imagine the experiences. Were the experiences enlightening or frightening? In what ways is an air balloon like a pond or a sunset? What other CONNECTIONS can be made with a balloon?

COAUTHORING

RULES:

1 Form writing teams of two students. Read or provide copies of "The Story," page 61, to each team. Each team is to read the page and then determine who will be the first coauthor and the second coauthor.

2 Each coauthor is to take turns adding to the story until the page is completed. During this period of time there should be no communication or cues given on how the story should be written. The page is simply passed back and forth to each author.

3 After completing the page, team members can converse on how their story should demonstrate continuity from what was written earlier. What was previously written on page 62 cannot be altered.

The

STORY

The sun, fading quickly, extended the shadows. Evening sounds began in the trees and a summer's day was ending. He looked to the emerging stars and pondered the concept of construction from destruction like so many others before him. Feeling good about being here, he stretched his legs and felt the support of the live oak against his back.

He came here with his problems like he had before, hoping not so much for a solution but to place things in some kind of perspective, some kind of order.

He gazed at the wood he had pyramided. Soon he would light it and the warmth would dry the dampness on which he sat. The bag would be unrolled, and he would sleep and awaken to the full brilliance of a night sky. And through the order of the tail end of this galaxy, called the Milky Way, he would look for some order in his own life. At some time after the owl's call and before the last remaining shadow, he slept. He had forgotten to light the fire.

There came a chilling breeze, and the leaves above him fluttered like the banners waving from an ancient marching army. He awoke to this and the flurry of birds in a frenzy of flight that deafened his ears. Stunned, he gathered himself to his knees and saw in the night sky a brilliant display of cosmic light.

A silence came like he had never known. The wind became still and there were no sounds within the forest.

And from the patch of pine, where he gathered firewood earlier, came a light, not of the kind in the skies, but a dancing, shimmering light of yellow and blue. Frightened, he gathered a piece of wood from the pyramid. He wanted to run and started to. But his body became limp and he felt the bark of the live oak against his sliding back as he fell uncontrollably to its base.

Take turns in completing "The Story."

1st coauthor _____

_____

_____

_____

_____

_____

2nd coauthor _____

_____

_____

_____

_____

_____

1st coauthor _____

_____

_____

_____

_____

2nd coauthor _____

_____

_____

_____

_____

Now decide together how "The Story" should end. Write the ending on a different sheet of paper.

EGG - O - MATIC

CULTIVATING: Creativity (elaboration and originality) and Empathy

Originality can be enhanced by encouragement and challenge. These two conditions make up a good portion of the atmosphere that is necessary for creative production.

Empathy to whatever we are addressing our attentions to allows for a greater openness and receptivity to other possibilities. Thus, empathy is a strong associate to the creative process.

The carry-over of the above is meeting life challenges in imaginative ways.

GETTING STARTED: In beginning the activity do not place any restrictions on what an egg-decorating machine must look like, be, or how it might function. It can be described in writing or drawn or developed in any combination thereof.

AFTERWARDS: After sharing the individual conceptions of an egg-decorating machine, CONNECT the uniqueness of the machine with the uniqueness of other forms. Try the CONNECTION of snowflakes and their individuality with the individuality of the human species.

For added effect and CONNECTIVENESS, pass out walnuts to your students. One walnut per student will do. Allow five minutes for everyone to study the grooves, shape, blemishes and any other characteristic noted. Take a paper sack and have students place their walnuts in it. Shake the sack and line up the walnuts on a table. Have students find their walnuts. This exercise will permeate a dramatic effect for talking about human sensitivity (empathy) in the observation of all things - sensitivity to self, to others and to events we come in contact with.

Now ask, "How is an egg-decorating machine like a walnut?"

"How is an egg-decorating machine and a walnut like a human being?"

63

EGG-O-MATIC

Design a deluxe egg-decorating machine.

MY GLURP

CULTIVATING: Valuing and Self-esteem

This activity could identify important values. In other words, when choosing, prizing, and acting upon a free choice, we feel better about things and ourselves. We tend to be consistent about our decision making and direction when these elements are involved.

GETTING STARTED: Tell the students that the letters G, L, U, R and P have meaning. "G" is for something you are good at; "L" is for something you like to do; "U" is for something you could do umpteen times without getting bored; "R" is for something that releases your energy and "P" stands for something you are proud of.

Have students think of something they do in which each letter within GLURP would fit.

Give an example of one of your own GLURPS or give this sample as an example:

"My GLURP is gathering seed pods, mushrooms, and unusual grasses and weeds which are preserved and pasted to strips of old barn siding. The strips make beautiful wall hangings. In fact, some of the wall hangings I give away. I feel very proud when I see my work in someone's house."

A GLURP can be almost anything that one prizes, enjoys, and feels proud about.

Encourage each student to bring a small photo of himself to class. Have the student paste his photo in the upper middle of the picture frame. It is not necessary for the student to draw the entire body; the upper portion or extremities will work fine.

AFTERWARDS: Have students share and discuss their GLURPS with one another. Engage your class in a discussion about what factors would make a GLURP a GLURP.

My GLURP

What's a GLURP? A **GLURP** is something you're good at; something you like; something you could do umpteen times without getting bored; something that releases your energy, and something you're proud of.

My GLURP is _____

_____

_____

_____

_____

Paste a class photo of you within the picture frame. Finish the picture by drawing yourself doing your GLURP!

66

LIST THINGS THAT WOULD
CAUSE YOUR KNEES TO WOBBLE

CULTIVATING: Empathy

The first step in conquering fear is to acknowledge it. Recognizing that others experience feelings similar to our own is important. We feel less alone when concerns have been expressed and shared.

GETTING STARTED: Before distributing the activity, talk about fear. Talk about things that cause fear.

AFTERWARDS: Encourage students to share "things that would cause their knees to wobble."

The important thing here is to air a wide variety of fears. A student who expresses a fear of making a class report will find others who share the same feeling. The simple acknowledgement that others have experienced similar feelings is an important CONNECTION - a strong, supportive statement. It's like saying, 'Hey, maybe I'm o.k. since others feel the way I do." Stronger fears will surface. Just acknowledge them as a normal condition, which they are.

The important thing with this activity is the identification with human feelings expressed by others.

Sometimes the best treatment for fear is truth.

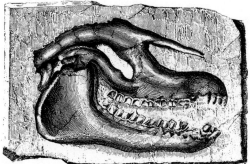

LIST THINGS THAT WOULD CAUSE YOUR KNEES TO WOBBLE

1 _____
2 _____
3 _____
4 _____
5 _____
6 _____
7 _____
8 _____
9 _____
10 _____
11 _____
12 _____
13 _____

My worst wobble would likely be no.____ because _____

_____
_____ .

MY COAT OF ARMS

CULTIVATING: Self-esteem and Empathy

Discovering those special kinds of things about ourselves and learning to appreciate them is the developing point for a healthy self-concept.

GETTING STARTED: Encourage discussion on how symbols are used in corporation logos or on football helmets for communicating messages. During the Middle Ages some families created coats of arms to describe family achievements, vocations, and beliefs.

Provide copies of the activity sheet to your class and write the following directions on the chalkboard:

1.   In space number 1, print your full name in a very special way.

2.   In space 2, express in a drawing something that would best describe you.

3.   In space number 3, express in a drawing something that might describe what you will be doing fifteen years from now.

4.   In space number 4, express in a drawing a very special wish or dream you have.

5.   In space number 5, express in a drawing a special achievement you achieved.

6.   In space number 6, express in a drawing a special memory or event in your life.

This activity can be done either at school or at home. Provide plenty of time and encourage students to make a very special coat of arms.

AFTERWARDS: Provide time for each student to describe his own coat of arms to the entire class. Display all coats of arms in the classroom.

MY COAT OF ARMS

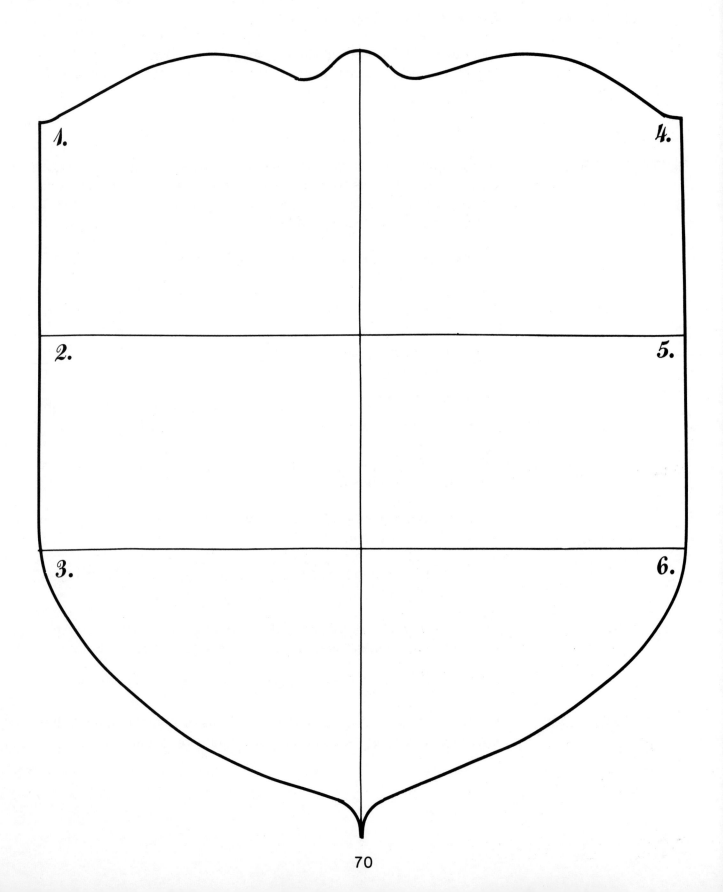

THE MISUNDERSTOOD MONSTER

CULTIVATING: Empathy and Creativity (originality)

To improve the human condition requires among other things empathy. Empathy is a learned trait, thus teachable.

GETTING STARTED: Encourage students to use their imaginations in creating a lovable monster story.

AFTERWARDS: In analyzing the stories, look for a sensitivity of style and purpose.

In analyzing for originality, look for surprising events and plots, the use of inventive words and phrases, and add-ons you didn't expect, like illustrations.

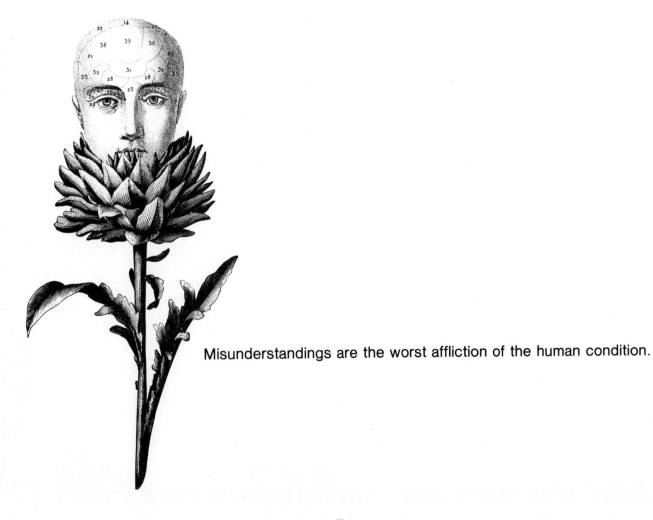

Misunderstandings are the worst affliction of the human condition.

Write a story about –

THE MISUNDERSTOOD MONSTER

Once upon a time...

BEAT A BUG

CULTIVATING: Empathy and Creativity (fluency)

Stress is the result of conditions or problems that seem to go beyond our control. Being empathetic and sensitive to ourselves and situations that can promote stress is crucial. Steps that follow may include the generation of alternative solutions, determining the best solution and acting on that choice.

GETTING STARTED: Tell students that today's exercise is a private exercise - one for their own benefit. Their responses will not be shared in class. Also indicate that if anyone would like to share the results of the activity with you, that's o.k!

The crucial element in the activity is the listing of ways for dealing with the problem. Encourage students to generate as many possibilities as possible on the backsides of the activity sheets. Have them think through the possible consequences of each choice. You might have them rank the consequences as being either excellent, o.k., or poor as a simple criteria. The "I will" statement should reflect the solution chosen.

AFTERWARDS: Provide time for individual counseling in the next several days. Also, from time to time, ask students in a general way if they have acted on their choices yet?

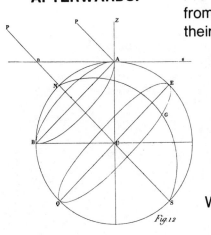

Without problems there wouldn't be challenges.

BEAT A BUG

* **Something** that really b**ugg**ed me was . . .

On another piece of paper list as many ways as you can for dealing with the thing that "bugged" you!

Make a prediction on the possible success of each way, then choose one.

I will . . .

A THREE-PERSON DRAWING

CULTIVATING: Cooperation

Conflict, coercion, and frustration are not characteristic of successful problem solving.

This exercise will likely generate all of the above behaviors. It is important to know the behaviors that are not conducive to the process or the product of cooperative effort.

GETTING STARTED: Arrange seating so that three persons are working together. Some groups may have two or four persons. This will be satisfactory for the purposes of the activity.

Go over the directions on the activity page with the students. They are:

"Without talking, take turns in drawing a group picture. Do not decide beforehand what the picture will be."

"Each person should not draw a line that would exceed the length: _____ . The lines can be curved or shaped in any way."

Emphasize to students that they are to try to transmit with their drawn lines ideas to their teammates concerning the group picture.

Provide about fifteen minutes of working time on this activity. Most groups will probably not complete the group drawing.

AFTERWARDS: Ask how many groups were able to complete the picture.

For those that did not, ask:

1.   How many of you felt frustrated?

2.   How many of you felt that an idea you didn't like was being forced on you?

3.   How many of you felt like quitting this exercise before I said stop?

Now think about this next question:

4.   What are the necessary elements of group cooperation?

75

A THREE-PERSON DRAWING

Begin here ➡

DIRECTIONS:

Without talking, take turns in drawing a group picture. Do not decide beforehand what the picture will be.

Each person should not draw a line that would exceed this length: _____ . The lines can be curved or shaped in any way.

LIST THINGS THAT ARE DIFFICULT TO SHARE

CULTIVATING: Valuing and Creativity (fluency and flexibility)

The basis of true friendship is the ability to share. When we really share, we share whatever good and bad qualities we have. Being accepted on those terms permeates the best and most lasting relationships.

GETTING STARTED: Begin this exercise by calling attention to the examples on the student activity page. A **STOMACHACHE** is difficult to share because most pain is an individual matter. **HAPPINESS** is also an individual thing. What makes one person happy isn't necessarily the same for another.

Provide about fifteen minutes for the written responses and an equal amount of time for discussion afterwards.

AFTERWARDS: Encourage students to share on a voluntary basis their responses. Ask how many items on their list CANNOT BE seen, touched, smelled, heard, or tasted? Chances are those items fitting the above criterion are feelings. Have students quietly think about how many people they know they would share these things with?

Use this teachable moment to discuss the concept of close friends. Discuss the need for all of us to have friendships of this kind. Having good friends to really share things with is very important.

Nothing is ever too difficult to share.

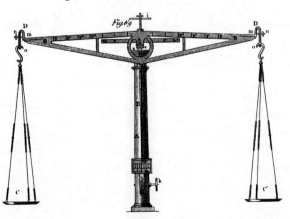

List Things

That Are Difficult to Share

a stomachache

happiness

CONNECTING RAINBOWS

CULTIVATING: Self-esteem

Doing something considerate and special for another person is important. It can build esteem for both the provider and the receiver.

Why connect a rainbow? **CONNECTING RAINBOWS** is both a visual and verbal acknowledgment to someone who did something special for you. That something special might have been an act of kindness, consideration or a few meaningful words. The message carries a warm meaning far more emphatic than just a "thank-you."

The rainbow symbol is an international message of harmony and peace. Use it for **CONNECTING** with inner harmony and peace.

GETTING STARTED: Run several copies of the memo and keep them on hand for frequent messages of goodwill to your students. Let them know when a special action on their part made your day a little better.

Do not create a special criteria for awarding the memo; just allow your feelings to dictate the occasions.

Occasionally provide the memo to the entire class on those special days. Chances are more special days will follow.

AFTERWARDS: After a few weeks of **CONNECTING RAINBOWS**, on your initiative, ask your students if they would like to have several copies of their own memos. If so, duplicate more and encourage students to use them among classmates, parents, and friends.

Finding the **CONNECTIONS** is what it's all about.

CONNECTING RAINBOWS

To:

From:

You connected my rainbow when

_____

_____

_____

_____

DIRECTIONS:

1. Duplicate several copies of this page.

2. Assemble a memo pad of messages by cutting along the dotted lines.

3. Create a message of goodwill by acknowledging special acts of kindness and thoughtfulness displayed by your students.

THE SUNSHINE SEMESTER EXAM

CULTIVATING: Valuing

Wondering about the whys and wherefores is one of the prime and beautiful characteristics of the human species, for without it there would be no improvement or discovery.

There are those who find themselves indifferent to the things around them. Encourage persons of this kind to wonder and see value in it, for in the long run we shall all suffer for not doing so.

GETTING STARTED: Like **THE SUNSHINE POP QUIZ**, distribute this activity at the close of a school day. Allow time for completion in a mutual sharing and giving way.

AFTERWARDS: Prior to the sharing of responses, establish that **NO COMMENTS** or **CRITICAL STATEMENTS** be made. All statements must be received in **SILENCE**.

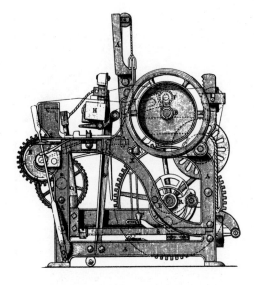

Great achievements trace their origins to,
"I wonder . . . . . "

THE SUNSHINE SEMESTER EXAM

name: _____ **date:** _____

Select an "I wonder" statement. Do another one if you'd like to!

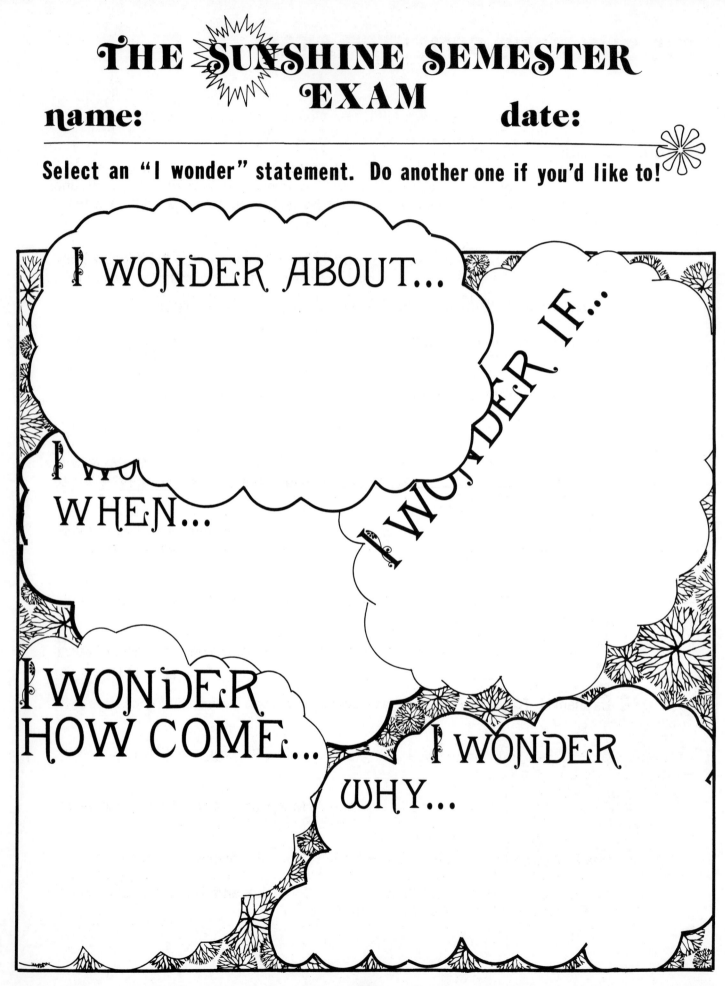

I WONDER ABOUT...

I WONDER IF...

I WONDER WHEN...

I WONDER WHY...

I WONDER HOW COME...

I WONDER WHY...

BIBLIOGRAPHY

Bloom, Benjamin S., (editor). **Taxonomy of Educational Objectives, Handbook I: Cognitive Domain.** New York: David McKay Company, Inc., 1956.

Borton, Terry. **Reach, Touch, and Teach.** New York: McGraw-Hill Book Company, 1970.

Eberle, Bob, and Hall, Rosie E. **Affective Education Guidebook.** Buffalo: D.O.K. Publishers, Inc., 1975.

Eberle, Bob, and Stanish, Bob. **CPS for Kids: A Resource Book for Teaching Creative Problem Solving to Children.** Buffalo: D.O.K. Publishers, Inc., 1980.

Glasser, William. **Schools Without Failure.** New York: Harper & Row, 1969.

Gowan, John Curtis. **Development of the Creative Individual.** San Deigo: Knapp Publishers, 1972.

Guilford, J. P. **Way Beyond the IQ.** Buffalo: The Creative Education Foundation, 1977.

Guilford, J. P. **The Nature of Human Intelligence.** New York: McGraw-Hill Book Company, 1967.

Harmin, Merrill, and Gregory, Tom. **Teaching Is.** Chicago: Science Research Associates, 1974.

Krathwohl, David R., Bloom, Benjamin S., and Masia, Bertram B. **Taxonomy of Educational Objectives, Handbook II: The Affective Domain.** New York: David McKay Company, Inc., 1964.

MacKinnon, Donald W. **In Search of Human Effectiveness, Identifying and Developing Creativity.** Buffalo: The Creative Education Foundation, 1978.

Maslow, Abraham H. **The Farther Reaches of Human Nature.** New York: The Viking Press, 1971.

Maslow, Abraham H. **Toward a Psychology of Being**. New York: D. Van Nostrand Company, 1968.

Noller, Ruth B. **Scratching the Surface of Creative Problem Solving, A Bird's Eye View of CPS.** Buffalo: D.O.K. Publishers, Inc., 1977.

Noller, Ruth B., Parnes, Sidney J., and Biondi, Angelo M. **Creative Actionbook**. Scribner's, 1976.

Osborn, Alex F. **Applied Imagination** (3rd Ed.). New York: Scribner's, 1963.

Raths, Louis E., Harmin, Merrill, and Simon, Sidney B. **Values and Teaching.** Columbus: Charles E. Merrill Publishing Company, 1966.

Read, Donald A., and Simon, Sidney B., (editors). **Humanistic Education Sourcebook.** Englewood Cliffs: Prentice-Hall, Inc., 1975.

Renzulli, Joseph S. **New Directions in Creativity,** Volumes Mark 1, Mark 2, and Mark 3. New York: Harper & Row, 1973.

Rogers, Carl R. **Freedom to Learn.** Columbus: Charles E. Merrill Publishing Company, 1969.

Simon, Sidney B., Howe, Leland W., and Kirschenbaum. **Values Clarification.** New York: Hart Publishing Company, Inc., 1972.

Stanish, Bob. **Hippogriff Feathers: Encounters with Creative Thinking.** Carthage, IL: Good Apple, Inc., 1981.

Stanish, Bob. **I Believe in Unicorns: Classroom Experiences for Activating Creative Thinking.** Carthage, IL: Good Apple, Inc., 1979.

Stanish, Bob. **Sunflowering: Thinking, Feeling, Doing Activities for Creative Expression.** Carthage, IL: Good Apple, Inc., 1977.

Stanish, Bob. **The Unconventional Invention Book: Classroom Activities for Activating Student Inventiveness.** Carthage, IL: Good Apple, Inc., 1981.

Torrance, E. Paul. **The Search for Satori and Creativity.** Buffalo: The Creative Education Foundation, 1979.

Vincent, William S. **Indicators of Quality, "Signs of Good Teaching."** Institute of Administrative Research, Teachers College, New York: Columbia University, 1969.

Williams, Frank E. **Classroom Ideas for Encouraging Thinking and Feeling.** Buffalo: D.O.K. Publishers, Inc., 1970.

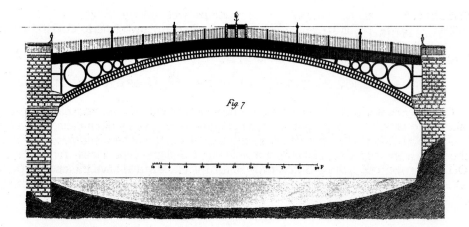

Fig. 7

THE GROWING FAMILY OF GOOD APPLE PRODUCTS INCLUDES:

☆ *PERIODICALS* . . . four to choose from . . . each will bring you a wealth of ideas.

★ **THE GOOD APPLE NEWSPAPER** . . . Ideas! Ideas! Ideas! That is what *The Good Apple Newspaper* is all about. Each issue, and there are five each school year, is a treasure-house of materials for the K-8 teacher. Games, posters, units of learning, task cards, bulletin board ideas, etc. Ideal for all subject areas, adaptable for all grade levels . . . innovative, skill-building, easy-to-use ideas for you and your students.

★ **LOLLIPOPS, LADYBUGS AND LUCKY STARS** . . . And you will thank your lucky stars for finding this newspaper of ideas and activities for teachers of preschool and primary children. Each year there are five 32-page issues chocked full of delightful learning experiences for early learners: patterns, poems, stories, readiness skills, reinforcement activities for all subject areas, arts and crafts, reading, music!

★ **CHALLENGE** . . . **reaching & teaching the GIFTED child**. . . for parents and teachers of gifted, talented and creative children of all ages. Our **CHALLENGE** at Good Apple is to put the world of gifted education at your fingertips-- identification, evaluation, methods of instruction, materials, model programs, units of study, mind benders--with the nation's prominent authorities in the field helping. Joe Wayman, editor.

RAINBOWS, DREAMS AND BUTTERFLY WINGS. . . an exciting religious education publication. Thirty-two cleverly illustrated pages of practical teaching techniques and suggestions for educators teaching in private schools, church programs and parents seeking materials for home use, including Bible quiz activities, creative writing, family worship, bulletin board ideas, posters, music-related fun, Biblical heroes, gameboards, arts, crafts. (K-8)

☆ *BOOKS*. . . over 150 titles in all subject areas for all grade levels, preschool - 8. Idea books, activity books, bulletin board books, units of instruction all with many reproducible pages.

READING	READINESS	VOCABULARY	SPELLING
BOOK REPORTS	DICTIONARY FUN	LANGUAGE ARTS	CREATIVE WRITING
CREATIVITY	GIFTED EDUCATION	BASIC SKILLS	STORYTELLING
GAMEBOARD IDEAS	POETRY	MATH (all areas)	METRICS
LEARNING CENTERS	CONTRACTS	OUTDOOR EDUCATION	INDEPENDENT STUDY
SCIENCE	SOCIAL STUDIES	SELF-CONCEPT	MEDIA-TELEVISION
ARTS/CRAFTS	PRESCHOOL	PRIMARY	MIDDLE SCHOOL
HOLIDAY IDEAS	BULLETIN BOARDS	TEACHER HELPERS	WORD GAMES
CAREER EDUCATION	PHYSICAL EDUCATION	HEALTH	AWARDS
MOTIVATION	MUSIC	ART EDUCATION	CLASSROOM ENVIRONMENT

GOOD APPLE MIGHT HAVE JUST THE VERY BOOK YOU HAVE BEEN LOOKING FOR!

★ **RECORDS -- CASSETTES** . . . a dozen favorites with accompanying activity books.
★ **ACTIVITY POSTERS** . . . over 30 titles each 17" x 22". Your students will love to complete them.
★ **NOTE PADS** . . . 2 dozen choices to reward and motivate. A note for almost every occasion.
★ **OTHER GOOD APPLE PRODUCTS INCLUDE** . . . films, T-shirts, bumper stickers, tote bags, note cards.

☆ *WORKSHOPS* . . . Good Apple will provide you with a unique variety of workshops, from gifted education to positive self-concept, from make-it and take-it to major content areas of curriculum. Twenty outstanding consultants are available to meet your needs. All of the Good Apple professionals are experienced teachers and recognized authorities. Our programs include scheduled workshops, special-purpose workshops designed specifically for your school and summer institutes where YOU will be the focus of a 3-5 day involvement experience and have the opportunity for graduate credit. We will work together on providing a workshop to fit your needs! Write to: Good Apple Workshops, Box 299, Carthage, IL 62321-0299 or call Bob Steinman at 217-357-3981.

FOR A FREE CATALOG WRITE: Good Apple, Inc., Box 299, Carthage, IL 62321-0299